staying
in love

falling in love is easy, staying in love requires a plan

PARTICIPANT'S GUIDE

Andy Stanley

 ZONDERVAN®

NORTH POINT RESOURCES

ZONDERVAN.com/
AUTHORTRACKER
follow your favorite authors

ZONDERVAN

Staying in Love Participant's Guide
Copyright © 2010 by North Point Ministries, Inc.

Requests for information should be addressed to:
Zondervan, *Grand Rapids, Michigan 49530*

ISBN 978-0-310-40861-1

All Scripture quotations, unless otherwise indicated, are taken from the Holy Bible, *Today's New International Version™, TNIV®*. Copyright © 2001, 2005 by Biblica, Inc.™ Used by permission of Zondervan. All rights reserved worldwide.

Italics in Scripture quotations are the author's emphasis.

Any Internet addresses (websites, blogs, etc.) and telephone numbers printed in this book are offered as a resource. They are not intended in any way to be or imply an endorsement by Zondervan, nor does Zondervan vouch for the content of these sites and numbers for the life of this book.

All rights reserved. No part of this publication may be reproduced, stored in a retrieval system, or transmitted in any form or by any means—electronic, mechanical, photocopy, recording, or any other—except for brief quotations in printed reviews, without the prior permission of the publisher.

Cover and interior design by Brian Manley (funwithrobots.com)

Printed in the United States of America

11 12 13 14 15 /DCI/ 20 19 18 17 16 15 14 13 12 11 10 9 8 7 6 5 4

CONTENTS

INTRODUCTION

Together Forever

by Andy Stanley

What does it take to fall in love?

Not much more than a pulse.

But what does it take to *stay* in love?

That's a profoundly   important question—one we all ask our-selves at some point. And rare as it seems to happen, staying in love over the long haul is an intense and inescapable desire for all of us.

Is It Even Possible?

In 2008, writer Diablo Cody won the Oscar for "Best Original Screen-play" for the movie *Juno*. The title character is a teenage girl, and in one of the film's most memorable and tender scenes, she confesses to her father, "I'm losing my faith in humanity." As he seeks clarifica-tion, she continues, "I just need to know that it's possible for two people to stay happy together forever."

Is it possible?

We all hold at least a glimmer of hope that it is—that our marriages will be everything we want them to be, everything they could be. We see ourselves together forever with that special someone we know and love like no other.

This craving for that *one* special relationship is rooted deep within us. Yeah, we've got our friends—our tennis partners, our fishing buddies, our pals at work, the people we go shopping or bowling or to the movies with. But that can never satisfy our longing for that one-on-one soul mate, that fall-in-love best friend, that one somebody special with whom we can share the deepest companionship and intimacy, lighting a spark with that person that stays kindled forever—the passion, the excitement, the romance. We don't want to just survive in marriage; we see ourselves *together* always and still enjoying each other as the years go by, still holding hands, even as we get old and our bodies change and the world transforms around us.

Even if I told you that finding that kind of relationship is impossible, and that you'll only waste your time shooting for it—it wouldn't stop you from looking. It's just *in* you to want that—it's a deep desire.

Looking Around for Help

Can we count on our culture to help us out in fulfilling that desire?

Well, our culture has at least made it easier than ever before to get connected in a relationship. Did you know there are over 1,500 organizations in this country that will take the "personal profile" you provide them (along with a fee) and then match you with someone with a similar profile?

So while it might be easier than ever to find someone to fall in love with, given the unspoken rules of love in our culture, it is nearly impossible to stay in love with that person. We quickly pick up on how it works: *Do unto others what they deserve. Do unto others as they do unto you. Do unto others as your mood would have it. Do unto others so they'll see things your way. Do unto others until you wear them down and they agree to your demands.* No wonder so many couples are just surviving in their relationships, if they're staying together at all.

Add that to our super-high expectations, our super-long lists of personal needs to be met by our partners, our super-low tolerance for disappointment, and our super-quick willingness to dump a relationship that isn't working and start over with someone else—and most of us find ourselves ill-equipped to sustain the kind of last-forever romantic relationship we long for. The odds are stacked against us.

Fortunately, the ancient book we call the Bible has so much to

say about the here and now—so much practical relevance to everything in our lives today, including our relationships. It has so much to
show and tell us about building the right foundation for love relationships that endure—and that's what we'll be exploring together in the
weeks ahead.

Find Out for Yourself

As we look at these guidelines for enduring relationships, don't take
my word for it. Find some couples who are happily married today
after twenty or thirty years or more—I know they can be hard to find
sometimes, but if you do find them, ask them about it. Let them tell
you about choices they made, and how they worked through their
marriage difficulties, and what they learned about being better people. I think you'll discover that what they tell you will only reinforce the
good things we'll be looking at together.

So let's start . . .

SESSION 1

Love Is a Verb

There's something in us that craves a relationship with that one special someone who knows us like no one else. We want that one person we can share life with, do life with . . . and *finish* life with.

I believe that this longing we all seem to have is just the thumbprint of God on our souls. It's a desire God placed in us, as part of our being created in his image. It makes us want to fall in love and stay in love with one person forever.

The *falling* in love part is easy enough—most of us have done it a number of times. But the staying in love . . . now that's another matter.

Glancing around at the marriages we know, and taking in what our culture tells us, we don't find much, if any, evidence for the kind of long-lasting relationships we crave.

So the question haunts us: *Is staying in love even possible?*

DISCUSSION STARTER

Think about the marriages of people you know best. What elements contributed to failed marriages? What elements contributed to lasting, long-term marriages?

VIDEO OVERVIEW

For Session 1 of the DVD

It's a fascinating question, profoundly important, and one that we all ask at some point: Is it possible for a husband and wife to stay in love—to stay happy together forever?

In spite of the troubled marriages we see all around us, most of us would answer, "Yes, it's possible." We even hold out hope that it's possible for us, a hope that reflects something of the image of God in us. We want a marriage where we as a couple finish together, and finish strong.

Yes, we affirm, it must be possible! But we aren't so sure that it is probable. We have our doubts about that.

Falling in love has never been easier, thanks in part to today's electronic social networking; but staying in love has never been more difficult. Few of us have been able to closely observe a fully healthy, romantic marriage relationship, and today's relational "rules" are self-centered and manipulative.

Meanwhile, the standards of what we expect from a relationship are as high as ever—we want massive doses of respect, encouragement, comfort, security, support, acceptance, approval, appreciation, attention, and affection. We come into a marriage feeling our own deficits in many of these areas, and expecting our spouse to make up for them.

Moreover, our culture has a very low threshold of relational pain. We're constantly told that if we find ourselves unhappy in a relationship, it's because we chose the wrong person, so now we need to abort that relationship and choose someone else.

Into that kind of relational chaos, Jesus has spoken. Two thousand years ago, he gave us the foundation for romantic love relationships that endure. This foundation is crystallized for us in the words of Jesus in John 13:34—"A new command I give you: Love one another. As I have loved you, so you must love one another."

It's simple, yet counterintuitive. Jesus takes this word *love*—which we normally perceive as a noun, something we fall into, or a feeling we experience—and he highlights it as a verb. It's something you do, an active choice you make. And once you do, then the feelings will follow. Making love a verb is the foundation for staying in love.

And Jesus asks us to take our cue in this from him—from his own love as he demonstrated it for us.

Years later, the apostle Paul amplified this idea of active love in terms of mutual submission in a marriage—where each partner gives priority to the other person. Our model in this is Christ, who gave his life while submitting to us and making our needs his priority.

VIDEO NOTES

_____

_____

_____

_____

_____

_____

_____

_____

_____

_____

_____

_____

_____

_____

_____

_____

_____

_____

_____

_____

_____

DISCUSSION QUESTIONS

1. If a young teenager asked *you* that question—"How possible is it for two people to stay happy together forever?"—how would you answer, and what reasons would you give for your answer? And how different is that from the way you might have answered, say, five years ago?

2. How realistic is it to hold out hope for that one romantic relationship that will stay full of passion and intimacy? How *right* is it?

3. Think of the relational habits promoted by our culture. Which ones have you noticed work against enduring love relationships?

4. When you recall that Jesus tells us to love one another *as he loved us,* what standards and guidelines for relationships does that bring to mind?

5. What typically keeps couples from practicing mutual submission in marriage, from always giving priority to the other person?

6. In Ephesians 5:21, we're told, "Submit to one another out of reverence for Christ." What do you think it means in a marriage to practice mutual submission *out of reverence for Christ*?

MILEPOSTS

- We all crave that one romantic relationship that will endure—and though we believe it's possible for us, we often have doubts about actually attaining it.

- In giving us the right foundation for an enduring relationship, Jesus teaches us to *make love a verb,* based on his own example.

- The biblical concept of lasting love, as modeled by Jesus, is one of *mutual submission* where each of us gives priority to the other in our daily decisions and actions.

MOVING FORWARD

"In our relationship, *you* are the priority"—these words might come fairly easy. What about the actions behind them?

In order to *make love a verb,* what are two or three action steps you can take immediately to demonstrate your decision to give first priority to your spouse?

CHANGING YOUR MIND

This session's key Scripture passage states the core dynamic behind "love as a verb," as expressed by Jesus:

A new command I give you: Love one another.
As I have loved you, so you must love one another.
John 13:34

Let these words motivate you to be proactive in loving your spouse, as you take your cues in this from Jesus himself.

PREPARATION FOR SESSION 2

To help you get ready for Session 2, use these suggested devotions during the week leading up to your small group meeting.

Day One

As your passage to focus on this week, read through Philippians 2:3–8, which gives relationship guidelines rooted in the life example of Jesus Christ. Notice especially verse 3. What makes these instructions difficult for most of us to carry out?

Day Two

Look closer at Philippians 2:4. Why do you think it's so important for married couples to make the effort to actively take notice of each other's personal interests—and even get involved in them?

Day Three

In verses 5–7 of Philippians 2, we're pointed to the example of Christ as the right standard for our own relationships with each other. From what you see in these verses, how would you describe the relational standards that Jesus demonstrated for us?

Day Four

Verse 8 in Philippians 2 tells us to what extent Jesus humbled himself for the sake of fulfilling God's plan for having a relationship with
us. How far did Jesus take it? And in our relationships with each
other, how far should we go in humbling ourselves for the sake of
one another?

Day Five

Read over again this week's passage, Philippians 2:3–8. How would
you summarize the uniqueness and radical difference in the relational guidelines that are taught here, as compared to the relational
guidelines we're more likely to learn from the culture around us?

Last Session

To experience the kind of lasting love relationship we all crave, the Bible teaches us to *make love a verb*—as each of us learns to give priority to the other.

SESSION 2

Re-Modeling

While falling in love requires only a pulse, *staying* in love requires a *plan*. Do you have one?

Most of us don't, so we can be grateful the Bible offers a set of helpful guidelines for exactly such a plan. It's the kind of strategy that requires something from us every day, something that touches on all our decisions and attitudes and actions. It may also require some radical new ways of thinking about yourself and about your spouse.

As a warm-up to this week's topic, think about the things we do in marriage that involve some measure of sacrifice for the sake of our spouses—coming home a bit earlier, saying thank you for a good meal, staying within our budgets, or taking the time and trouble to honestly share our feelings.

Now compare that with what the Bible tells us is the extent to which Jesus went to demonstrate his love for us: "he humbled himself by becoming obedient to death—even death on a cross!" (Philippians 2:8). That's how far Jesus went! And while showing us that, the Bible also says, "In your relationships with one another, have the same attitude of mind Christ Jesus had" (2:3). That's an inspiring standard, well worth a closer look.

DISCUSSION STARTER

From what you recall of the life of Jesus, what stands out most to you as an indication of his selflessness, his humility, and his dedication to serve others?

VIDEO OVERVIEW

For Session 2 of the DVD

A few years after Jesus taught his followers to love each other as he himself loved them, the apostle Paul built on that command and taught us more about this kind of active love as modeled by Christ. In Philippians 2:3–8, Paul said that we're to remove any element of competitiveness from our relationships, and to instead value our spouses as being more valuable and more important than we are. This attitude should govern our daily decisions and reactions.

Although we quickly resist this idea of constantly treating our spouses this way, the fact is, *all* of us want to be treated that way ourselves. And the married couples that *stay* in love over the long haul are those who've learned to treat each other with this respect, continually deferring to one another's wishes.

Paul goes on to say that we're to give focused attention to whatever our spouses are interested in, even if it holds no interest for us.

We're to approach all our relationships, Paul reminds us, in the same way Jesus approached his relationship with us. This gives us an entirely new way of relating to our husbands or wives.

For example, wherever Jesus was, he was always the most important person there—yet he never leveraged that for his own advantage, though he had every right to. Paul says that's how we must relate to each other. We're not to demand our way, but instead to be mutually submissive.

Focusing again on Christ's example, Paul describes how Jesus "made himself nothing" [or "emptied himself," as some Bible versions express it] by taking the very nature of a servant" (2:7). In his life on earth, Jesus didn't demand to be treated as God, but instead chose to serve others. He fully carried out this principle, all the way to death on a cross—all for the sake of a relationship with us!

Jesus knew he couldn't have it both ways; he couldn't hold on to his rank in heaven and yet also gain a lasting relationship with us.

He knew that our forgiveness from sin was our greatest need, and

he gave up his rights and priorities in order to meet that need for us.

In the same way, we can't have it both ways in marriage; if we

hold on to our rights and to what we think we deserve, we sacrifice

the quality and intimacy of our relationships. Instead, we need to

adopt the same attitude Jesus had, because this is what facilitates

deeper love and dedication in marriage.

VIDEO NOTES

DISCUSSION QUESTIONS

1. As you think about the marriages of people you know, in
    what ways have you seen "selfish ambition" or competitive-
    ness occur between the husbands and wives? What seems
    to be the cause of this?

2. In Philippians 2, we're told to humbly value others above
    ourselves—to actually see them as being more important
    than we are. Why is that so hard to actually practice? How
    can we get over the difficulty of it?

3. How important is mutual *respect* in a marriage, and what
    are some practical ways it should be demonstrated?

4. In your opinion, what kind of sharing of interests is best and healthiest for a marriage? What is the practical meaning of the relational guideline in Philippians 2:4 that we're to look not only to our own interests but also to the other person's interests?

5. Why is a 50/50 "contract" approach to marriage so detrimental to a lasting love relationship?

6. In a marriage, why is it impossible to pursue *both* an enduring love relationship *and* one's own rights and preferences? Why won't this work?

MILEPOSTS

- The Bible has much to say to us about how to *make love a verb*, especially in the approach to relationships that Jesus modeled for us.

- Mutual submission in marriage means getting rid of competitiveness and not demanding our own way. It means valuing the other person as more important than ourselves.

- If we try to hold on to our "rights" and what we think we deserve, we put our relationships at risk. We can't pursue our rights at the same time we pursue a deeper love in our relationships. We have to choose one or the other.

MOVING FORWARD

Based on Christ's model of humility in Philippians 2:3–8, there should be a "sense of awe" in our relationships, especially toward our spouses. What factors about your spouse are truly awe-inspiring?

Be specifically conscious of these things as you consider practical ways to demonstrate a new commitment to value your spouse above yourself. What can you do immediately as a genuine expression of your decision to treat your spouse as more important than yourself?

CHANGING YOUR MIND

Embrace these New Testament words from Paul as the right set of

foundational guidelines for your marriage relationship:

> *Do nothing out of selfish ambition or vain conceit.*
> *Rather, in humility value others above yourselves,*
> *not looking to your own interests*
> *but each of you to the interests of the others.*
> *In your relationships with one another,*
> *have the same attitude of mind Christ Jesus had.*
> *Philippians 2:3–5*

PREPARATION FOR SESSION 3

To help you get ready for Session 3, use these suggested devotions during the week leading up to your small group meeting.

Day One

Look at Proverbs 4:23. According to this passage, why is it so important to know the spiritual and emotional condition of our hearts?

Day Two

Listen to the words of Jesus in Matthew 5:19. How do these words reinforce the importance of knowing what's going on inside you?

Day Three

Listen to David's prayer in the final two verses of Psalm 139. Adapt this prayer in your own words as you seek God's help in understanding your heart.

Day Four

Look at the statement made in Psalm 119:32. The picture is one of freedom and power that comes from obeying God. What makes this freedom and power possible, according to this verse? And what might that mean practically for your life?

Day Five

Once more, focus on the words of Proverbs 4:23. What can you do to

protect your heart, spiritually and emotionally? What does it need to

be protected from?

Last Session

We can't have it both ways; if we give priority to pursuing deeper love and closeness in our relationships, it means no longer giving priority to our own rights and needs and preferences.

SESSION 3

Feelin' It

How is that two people can stand at an altar and swear on their lives that they'll love each other forever, "till death do us part"—and then absolutely hate each other only five years down the road? Not just that, but they hate each other more than any other individual on the planet. Isn't that weird?

Or think about this: Why is there even such a thing as "domestic violence"? Those two words shouldn't even be together. *Domestic* means "home"— where we live together, laugh together, raise children together. *Violence* means "hurt," in a terrible way. Why should there ever be a thing like that in a home?

And here's something else that begs an explanation: If you know two people who are getting divorced, and you ask why, they'll probably say they don't love each other anymore; they were once in love, but no longer. And if you then ask, "Do you think you'll be in love with someone again in the future?" they'll probably both answer yes.

Now suppose you tell them, "Here's a great idea: Why don't you just fall in love with *each other* again?" They'll probably say, "You don't understand; it's not that simple."

They're right; it's not that simple. But why isn't it?

Let's search together for some answers.

DISCUSSION STARTER

Among married people whom you know well, how do you see *emotions* having the biggest impact in their marriages? What kind of power and impact do emotions have in determining the quality of our relationships in marriage?

VIDEO OVERVIEW

For Session 3 of the DVD

As we've talked about love-as-a-verb and mutual submission as the way to stay in love in a marriage, you may have thought, "Yeah, but it's not that simple."

No, it isn't.

Although it *would* be that simple if we all came into marriage with backgrounds filled only with healthy relationships. Yet none of us do. We all bring baggage from relational hurts in our pasts. And that baggage will inescapably influence the way we experience our marriages. The emotional residue and repercussions from these difficult experiences in our pasts will inevitably spill out in the present as we hit various "bumps" in our marriage relationships.

That's why we're given these words of wisdom in the Bible: "Above all else, guard your heart, for everything you do flows from it" (Proverbs 4:23). We guard our hearts by paying careful attention to what's going on inside us.

We need a proactive strategy for doing this. We're good at monitoring our spouses' behavior, but we're horrible at monitoring what's really happening in our own hearts.

We learn to monitor our spouses' behavior because of a belief that this is what determines our own emotional satisfaction in the marriage. We fail to realize how much the condition of our own hearts determines that satisfaction. A healthy, intimate marriage relationship is impossible without our hearts being in good shape. That's why we have to monitor them.

A simple exercise can help us learn to pay better attention to what's inside us. Here are the steps for applying it to our relational encounters:

1. Before you speak, think about what you're actually feeling.

2. Identify this emotion or reaction by name (you feel *angry*, for example, or *embarrassed, unappreciated, unlovable, lonely, abandoned, afraid, out of control, betrayed, picked on, jealous, disrespected, insecure*).

3. Once you've identified it, say the name aloud.

4. If and when appropriate, tell your partner how you feel. And when your partner does this, the right way to respond is to simply say, "Thank you, I'm glad you told me."

As we learn to do this, we so often realize that a "marriage problem" we're experiencing is actually a problem in our own hearts.

This approach is effective because when healthy people discover that something they do or say elicits negative emotions in their partners, they learn to stop doing it.

VIDEO NOTES

_____

_____

_____

_____

_____

_____

_____

_____

_____

_____

_____

_____

_____

_____

_____

_____

_____

_____

_____

_____

DISCUSSION QUESTIONS

1. In the marriages of people you know, what are the typical kinds of baggage from the past that seem to surface unexpectedly?

2. In a situation where there may be conflict or hurt in a marriage, why is it so important to first understand what's going on in our own hearts?

3. In what ways have you found yourself monitoring your spouse's behavior in regard to situations involving potential conflict or disappointment?

4. What can help us to more clearly understand the baggage from our pasts as it impacts our marriages today? What can help us not ignore it or suppress it?

5. What can help us be more accepting of the fact that the "marriage problems" we encounter are very often individual "heart problems" that we need to identify, understand, and face up to?

6. There is a sense of freedom that comes when we finally identify the emotional baggage that we've brought into our relationships. Can you sense how attractive and enjoyable that freedom would be? What do you think it would typically lead to in a marriage relationship?

MILEPOSTS

- As we pursue an enduring love relationship, the baggage we bring into the relationship inescapably influences us. These things *will* surface as we encounter "bumps" in our marriages.

- That's why it's so important to "guard our hearts"—to be fully aware of what's going on inside us.

- In every potentially tough situation in our relationships, it's good to fully identify and name exactly what we're feeling— then to talk about this with our spouses, if and when appropriate.

MOVING FORWARD

Those "bump" situations occur regularly in our marriages—sometimes daily. When the next one comes in your marriage, be prepared to follow this exercise—(1) identify what you're feeling, (2) name it, (3) say the name aloud, and (4) if and when appropriate, talk about it with your spouse.

To help prepare for this, visualize in your mind a typical "bump" situation in your marriage, and imagine yourself responding by proceeding through each of these steps. Simply doing this in your mind ahead of time may reveal something about your emotions that you haven't fully addressed before.

CHANGING YOUR MIND

Let these urgent words from the Bible be a continuing reminder of

how critically important it is to realize what's going on inside you:

Above all else, guard your heart,
for everything you do flows from it.
Proverbs 4:23

PREPARATION FOR SESSION 4

To help you get ready for Session 4, use these suggested devotions during the week leading up to your small group meeting.

Day One

Review how love is described in the well-known words of 1 Corinthians 13:4–6. Which of these characteristics of love seem to be most powerful and influential in how they affect your marriage relationship?

Day Two

Focus on 1 Corinthians 13:7 and the four active expressions of love that are stated there. Focus especially on the *first* phrase on the list—how would you express it in your own words? And how does it demonstrate itself in attitudes and actions?

Day Three

Focus again on 1 Corinthians 13:7, this time on the *second* phrase on the list. How would you express it in your own words? And how does it demonstrate itself in attitudes and actions?

Day Four

Now focus on the *third* phrase on the list in 1 Corinthians 13:7. How would you express it in your own words? And how does it demonstrate itself in attitudes and actions?

Day Five

Once more, look at 1 Corinthians 13:7 and the four active expressions of love that are stated there. This time, focus especially on the *final* phrase on that list. How would you express it in your own words? And how does it demonstrate itself in attitudes and actions?

Last Session

Romantic relationships are where we get "bumped" the hardest, bringing to the surface the baggage from our pasts. Learning to stay in love requires that we fully understand what's going on in our hearts . . . and squarely facing it.

SESSION 4

Multiple Choice Marriage

The Bible's well-known "love chapter" is found in 1 Corinthians 13, and you've probably heard it read at weddings. Maybe you've even thought about what it says and even evaluated your own marriage role by these words from the apostle Paul. Maybe you've graded yourself along these lines . . .

Love is patient. Yep, got that. *Love is kind.* Check. *It does not envy.* Okay, that makes sense. *It does not boast.* Yeah, there's definitely no need to be arrogant. *It is not proud.* That's right, pride can be a problem relationally; gotcha, Paul, I'm with you on that. *It does not dishonor others.* Right. Not a good idea in a relationship to dishonor the other person. *It is not self-seeking.* Yeah, that works against love for sure. *It is not easily angered.* Okay, anger issues. We all have some of those, I guess. Going to work on that one. It *keeps no record of wrongs.* There's a big one. We probably all need to work on that. *Love does not delight in evil but rejoices with the truth.* That means you celebrate the win, you don't camp out on the mistakes.

Yeah, Paul, that's a good list.

Then we get to verse 7 in this description of love: *It always protects, always trusts, always hopes, always perseveres.* Or maybe we read some of the other Bible versions that express it this way: *Love bears all things, believes all things, hopes all things, endures all things.*

Whoa. We might have a problem with that set. Doesn't it kind of ignore reality? And that can't be a good thing, can it?

Or can it?

Let's find out more.

DISCUSSION STARTER

Has your definition of *love* changed any over the years? If so, how?

VIDEO OVERVIEW

For Session 4 of the DVD

The Bible's "love chapter"—1 Corinthians 13—contains many statements that all of us would agree are good guidelines for our relationships. But later in that passage comes a four-part statement that looks, on the surface, like unsound advice. And yet these four statements go together to communicate an extremely powerful concept in our marriages.

In that four-part statement, the apostle Paul says that love "always protects, always trusts, always hopes, always perseveres" (1 Corinthians 13:7). Yet doesn't that make love blind? Wouldn't that approach lead to unhealthy things like codependence in a relationship? Shouldn't we instead face up to reality?

But Paul is giving us a trustworthy way to respond to the disappointments we will inevitably face in our relationships.

All of us have expectations about our marriage partners, and we'll all constantly experience "gaps" where those expectations aren't met. Each time we do, we face a choice: In our minds and hearts, will we assume the worst about our spouses . . . or believe the best?

Husbands and wives who *stay in love* for the long haul learn to always assume the best, either by force of habit or by intuition. By doing so, they create an "upward spiral of love" leading to greater and greater intimacy.

But if we consistently assume the worst about our spouses when we face those gaps—and the gaps will always be there—that, too, is a cycle that feeds on itself. We start to be more about winning "points" and winning arguments, not realizing that with every such victory we sacrifice the long-term health of the relationship. We become willing participants in the demise of our marriages, regardless of who's "right" or "wrong" in the conflict.

All of us in our marriages are constantly making this choice, one way or the other.

The fact is, healthy people really do *not* want to disappoint their partners in any relationship. But when one partner assumes the worst when there's a gap in meeting expectations, the one partner starts feeling that it's impossible to please the other.

In contrast, by believing the best of each other, we create margin in the relationship where there's plenty of room to grow and improve and mature. "Gaps" can be used to leverage love and to draw spouses closer and closer together—because all our hearts are drawn toward environments of acceptance.

VIDEO NOTES

_____

_____

_____

_____

_____

_____

_____

_____

_____

_____

_____

_____

_____

_____

_____

_____

_____

_____

DISCUSSION QUESTIONS

1. In every relationship there are gaps between what we expect of the other person and how that person actually behaves. Why is that universally true? What's the root cause of these gaps?

2. In a typical marriage, how conscious are we of these gaps when we encounter them? And how often would you say these gaps occur in a typical marriage?

3. What do you think are some of the most common gaps that wives see in their husbands' behavior? And what are some of the most common gaps that husbands see in their wives' behavior?

4. Why is it so healthy and enriching to the relationship to be-
    lieve the best about our spouses when we encounter one
    of those gaps?

5. Why is it so unhealthy and harmful to the relationship when
    we choose to assume the worst about our spouses when
    we encounter one of those gaps?

6. What do you think are the most important factors in deter-
    mining whether we believe the best or assume the worst
    when we encounter these gaps in our spouses?

MILEPOSTS

- We all face "gaps" in our relationships where the other person doesn't fully meet our expectations.

- We'll stay in love if we learn to always assume the best about each other when we encounter those disappointments. This triggers an "upward spiral of love" leading to greater and greater intimacy.

- If we instead choose to believe the worst about our partners, we'll only spiral downward in the relationship.

MOVING FORWARD

Make this personal: What *to you* are the most powerful reasons for believing the best about your spouse when you encounter those inevitable gaps between your expectations and your spouse's behavior? Think of as many good reasons as possible, and write them down. Keep this list handy, and review it often to remind you of the right way to respond to those gaps.

Also take a moment to envision what you want your relationship with your spouse to look and feel like years down the road, as you both grow in the habit of believing the best about each other.

CHANGING YOUR MIND

This verse highlights the most important habits and practices in any

love relationship:

> *[Love] always protects, always trusts,*
> *always hopes, always perseveres.*
> *1 Corinthians 13:7*

Memorize this verse and hold on to it as a constant reminder to be-

lieve the best about your husband or wife.

Leader's Guide

So, You're the Leader...

Is that intimidating? Perhaps exciting? No doubt you have some mental pictures of what it will look like, what you will say, and how it will go. Before you get too far into the planning process, there are some things you should know about leading a small group discussion. We've compiled some tried and true techniques here to help you.

Basics About Leading

1. Cultivate discussion — It's also easy to think that the meeting lives or dies by your ideas. In reality, what makes a small group meeting successful are the ideas of everyone in the group. The most valuable thing you can do is to get people to share their thoughts. That's how the relationships in your group will grow and thrive. Here's a rule: The impact of your study material will typically never exceed the impact of the relationships through which it was studied. The more meaningful the relationships, the more meaningful the study. In a sterile environment, even the best material is suppressed.

2. Point to the material — A good host or hostess gets the party going by offering delectable hors d'oeuvres and beverages. You too should be ready to serve up "delicacies" from the material. Sometimes you will simply read the discussion questions and invite everyone to respond. At other times, you may encourage others to share their ideas. Remember, some of the best treats are the ones your guests will bring to the party. Go with the flow of the meeting, and be ready to pop out of the kitchen as needed.

3. Depart from the material — We have carefully designed this study for your small group. But that doesn't mean you should follow every part word for word. Knowing how and when to depart from the material is a valuable art. Nobody knows more about your people than you do. The narratives, questions, and exercises are here to provide a framework for discovery. However, every group is motivated differently. Sometimes the best way to start a small group discussion is simply to ask, "Does anyone have a personal insight or revelation you'd like to share from this week's material?" Then sit back and listen.

4. Stay on track — Although this may seem contradictory to the previous point, there is an art to facilitating an engaging conversation. While you want to leave some space for your group members to process the discussion, you need to keep your objectives in mind. If your goal is to have a meaningful experience with this material, then you should make sure the discussion is contributing to that end. It's easy to get off on a tangent. Be prepared to interject politely and refocus the group. You may need to say something like, "Excuse me, we're obviously all interested in this subject; however, I just want to make sure we cover all the material for this week."

5. Above all, pray — The best communicators are the ones that manage to get out of God's way enough to let him communicate *through* them. That's important to keep in mind. Books don't teach God's Word; neither do sermons nor group discussions. God himself speaks into the hearts of men and women, and prayer is our vital channel to communicate directly with him. Cover your efforts in prayer. You don't just want God present at your meeting; you want him to direct it.

We hope you find these suggestions helpful. And we hope you enjoy leading this study. You will find additional guidelines and suggestions for each session in the Leader's Guide notes that follow.

Leader's Guide
Session Notes

Session 1 — Love Is a Verb

Bottom Line

The biblical way toward an enduring love relationship—as modeled by Jesus himself—is to *make love a verb*. That means practicing mutual submission, giving priority to the other person in our daily decisions and actions.

Discussion Starter

Use the "Discussion Starter" printed in Session 1 of the Participant's Guide to "break the ice"—and to help everyone see that lasting romantic love is by no means guaranteed or even likely.

Video Overview

The Video Overview section for Session 1 will help group members identify certain themes or questions before they watch the DVD clip. As leader, you may choose to read or summarize this section for the group, or have a volunteer read it.

If you haven't done so already, at this point insert the DVD and choose Session 1 from the Group Curriculum menu options.

Notes for Discussion Questions

1. **If a young teenager asked *you* that question— "How possible is it for two people to stay happy together forever?"—how would you answer, and what reasons would you give for your answer? And how different is that from the way you might have answered, say, five years ago?**

    Your group's answers to this question will likely reinforce the personal significance we all attach to the *Juno* question. Allow plenty of time here for everyone to answer this.

2. **How realistic is it to hold out hope for that one romantic relationship that will stay full of passion and intimacy? How *right* is it?**

    You may want to help the group recall content from the DVD teaching to the effect that however unrealistic this hope sometimes seems, it is nevertheless *right*—and a reflection of God's image within us.

3. **Think of the relational habits promoted by our culture. Which ones have you noticed work *against* enduring love relationships?**

The answers here may repeat some of the DVD teaching content about our culture's unhealthy relational rules, as well as go beyond that.

4. **When you recall that Jesus tells us to love one another *as he loved us*, what standards and guidelines for relationships does that bring to mind?**

Help the group members reflect fully on the kind of life Jesus lived, as well as his sacrificial death on our behalf.

5. **What typically keeps couples from practicing mutual submission in marriage, from always giving priority to the other person?**

Allow plenty of time for everyone to answer this and to uncover our many self-centered actions and attitudes that hinder love and mutual submission.

6. **In Ephesians 5:21, we're told, "Submit to one another out of reverence for Christ." What do you think it means in a marriage to practice mutual submission** *out of reverence for Christ?*

    Help guide the discussion toward the constant value of staying Christ-centered in our marriages, and staying fully submitted to Christ's authority and example.

Moving Forward

Encourage your group members to take *deliberate* actions that will demonstrate their fresh commitment to give priority to their spouses.

Preparation for Session 2

Remember to point out the brief daily devotions that the group members can complete and that will stimulate discussion in your next session. These devotions will enable everyone to dig into the Bible and start wrestling with the topics that will come up next time.

Session 2 — Re-Modeling

Bottom Line

We can be grateful that the Bible carefully details for us the kind of Christlike humility, submission, and servanthood that allows us to achieve a love that endures.

Discussion Starter

Use the "Discussion Starter" listed for Session 2 of the Participant's Guide. This one should help everyone in your group focus on Jesus as our most worthy model of enduring love.

Video Overview

The Video Overview section for Session 2 will help group members identify certain themes or questions before they watch the DVD clip. As leader, you may choose to read or summarize this section for the group, or have a volunteer read it.

If you haven't done so already, at this point insert the DVD and choose Session 2 from the Group Curriculum menu options.

Notes for Discussion Questions

1. **As you think about the marriages of people you know, in what ways have you seen "selfish ambition" or competitiveness occur between the husbands and wives? What seems to be the cause of this?**

   Encourage the group members to also share ways in which they've seen this occur in their own marriages.

2. **In Philippians 2, we're told to humbly value others above ourselves—to actually see them as being more important than we are. Why is that so hard to actually practice? How can we get over the difficulty of it?**

   You may want to have someone read aloud Philippians 2:3–8 while everyone thinks about their answers to this question.

3. **How important is mutual *respect* in a marriage, and what are some practical ways it should be demonstrated?**

   In some ways, in practical terms, husbands may view respect differently than wives do.

4. **In your opinion, what kind of sharing of interests is best and healthiest for a marriage? What is the practical meaning of the relational guideline in Philippians 2:4 that we're to look not only to our own interests but also to the other person's interests?**

Encourage the group to think about the deepest and most significant "interests" we have, rather than more superficial involvements such as hobbies, personal tastes in entertainment, etc.

5. **Why is a 50/50 "contract" approach to marriage so detrimental to a lasting love relationship?**

A relationship truly based on love is more like 100/100 than 50/50.

6. **In a marriage, why is it impossible to pursue *both* an enduring love relationship *and* one's own rights and preferences? Why won't this work?**

The goal here is to help the group members articulate the reasons given in the DVD teaching content, as well as to possibly come up with additional reasons on their own.

You may want to conclude the discussion by emphasizing God's desires for all of us to experience enduring love in our marriages. That's why he has given us these rich relational guidelines in the Bible.

Moving Forward

The goal here is to help group members gain a clearer view of their spouses' special qualities and giftedness and character, and to therefore appreciate their spouses more than ever. This will lend greater reality and appropriateness to their effort to value their spouses above themselves.

Preparation for Session 3

Again, encourage your group members to complete the brief daily devotions. These will help stimulate discussion in your next session. They'll enable everyone to dig into the Bible and start wrestling with the topics coming up next time.

Session 3 — Feelin' It

Bottom Line

To stay in love forever, we have to fully understand what's going on in our hearts—and face it squarely when it comes to the surface through the "bumps" in our relationships.

Discussion Starter

Again, use the "Discussion Starter" listed for Session 3 of the Participant's Guide. This should help the group focus on the inescapable influence in marriage of the emotional residue from our backgrounds.

Video Overview

The Video Overview section for Session 3 will help group members identify certain themes or questions before they watch the DVD clip. As leader, you may choose to read or summarize this section for the group, or have a volunteer read it.

If you haven't done so already, at this point insert the DVD and choose Session 3 from the Group Curriculum menu options.

Notes for Discussion Questions

1. **In the marriages of people you know, what are the typical kinds of baggage from the past that seem to surface unexpectedly?**

   A wide variety of answers are possible and even likely here. By mentioning the kind of baggage you've recognized from your own past, you'll encourage the group members to do the same.

2. **In a situation where there may be conflict or hurt in a marriage, why is it so important to first understand what's going on in our own hearts?**

   It may be good here to bring in Proverbs 4:23, as the DVD teaching content does.

3. **In what ways have you found yourself monitoring your spouse's behavior in regard to situations involving potential conflict or disappointment?**

   Take the lead in answering this one transparently.

4. **What can help us to more clearly understand the baggage from our pasts as it impacts our marriages today? What can help us to not ignore it or suppress it?**

This might lead naturally into the exercise suggested in the DVD teaching content. Encourage the group members in this direction.

5. **What can help us be more accepting of the fact that the "marriage problems" we encounter are very often individual "heart problems" that we need to identify, understand, and face up to?**

The goal here is to help the group members grow in taking personal responsibility and ownership in regards to the baggage we bring into our marriages. If you can share how a marriage struggle enabled you to finally see a particular heart problem of your own, this can have a powerful effect on your group.

6. **There is a sense of freedom that comes when we finally discern emotional baggage that we've brought into our relationships. Can you sense how attractive and enjoyable that freedom would be? What do you think it would typically lead to in a marriage relationship?**

Guide the group in gaining an enticing vision of the release and strength and greater relational richness that's made possible as we effectively identify and deal with our baggage from the past.

Moving Forward

The value here is in helping the group members learn to consciously stop and carefully evaluate their spiritual and emotional heart conditions whenever a "bump" situation occurs. Remind them of how valuable this habit will become.

Preparation for Session 4

Again, encourage your group members to complete the daily devotions. This will help them be better prepared for the topics coming up next time.

Session 4 — Multiple Choice Marriage

Bottom Line

We face the choice repeatedly in our marriages: Believe the best about our spouses (and see our love deepen); or assume the worst (and watch our love wither).

Discussion Starter

Again, use the "Discussion Starter" listed for Session 4 of the Participant's Guide. This should help everyone focus on our need to conform our view of love to a biblical perspective.

Video Overview

The Video Overview section for Session 4 will help group members identify certain themes or questions before they watch the DVD clip. As leader, you may choose to read or summarize this section for the group, or have a volunteer read it.

If you haven't done so already, at this point insert the DVD and choose Session 4 from the Group Curriculum menu options.

Notes for Discussion Questions

1. **In every relationship there are gaps between what we expect of the other person and how that person actually behaves. Why is that universally true? What's the root cause of these gaps?**

    Despite the universality of this principle, most of us still find ourselves surprised by the reality of it at some point in our marriages.

2. **In a typical marriage, how conscious are we of these gaps when we encounter them? And how often would you say these gaps occur in a typical marriage?**

    It will be helpful if you can relate how you became more aware of these gaps in your own marriage—especially if you can also share how you came to recognize the kinds of disappointments you brought by not meeting your spouse's expectations.

3. **What do you think are some of the most common gaps that wives see in their husbands' behavior? And what are some of the most common gaps that husbands see in their wives' behavior?**

    This could spark a lively discussion. When it comes to experiencing these gaps, it will be good for each couple to realize afresh that "it's not just us"—rather, this is something we all face, all the time.

4. **Why is it so healthy and enriching to the relationship to believe the best about our spouses when we encounter one of those gaps?**
    Encourage the group to recall the reasons given in the DVD teaching content, as well as to identify additional reasons of their own.

5. **Why is it so unhealthy and harmful to the relationship when we choose to assume the worst about our spouses when we encounter one of those gaps?**
    Again, encourage the group to recall the reasons given in the DVD teaching content, as well as to identify additional reasons of their own.

6. **What do you think are the most important factors in determining whether we believe the best or assume the worst when we encounter these gaps in our spouses?**
    You may want to encourage the group to think about the trustworthiness of the relational guidelines given in God's Word, the glorious power of love as evidenced in the life and death of Jesus, and the sacredness that all human beings possess from

being created by God in his own image.

As you close, pray together as a group, and ask each person to offer a sentence prayer of gratitude for his or her spouse and for God's grace and wisdom in bringing them together in marriage.

Moving Forward

Be prepared to help the group members fill out their list by reminding them of the many reasons Andy gives in his message for always believing the best about our spouses.

Your Move

Four Questions to Ask When You Don't Know What to Do

Andy Stanley

We are all faced with decisions that we never anticipated having to make. And, we usually have to make them quickly. In this four session video group study, author and pastor Andy Stanley discusses four questions that will help participants make sound decisions with God's help. Follow Andy as he teaches how every decision and its outcomes become a permanent part of your story, what to do when you feel the need to pause before taking action, and how to make more of this life by making sound decisions.

The DVD-ROM and separate participant's guide contain everything you need to create your group experience:

Available in stores and online!

Faith, Hope, and Luck

Discover What You Can Expect from God

Andy Stanley

Our faith in God often hinges on his activity—or inactivity—in our daily experiences. When our prayers are answered, our faith soars. When God is silent, it becomes harder to trust him. When God shows up in an unmistakable way, our confidence in him reaches new heights. But when he doesn't come through, our confidence often wanes.

But it doesn't have to be that way—it's not supposed to be that way.

This five-session study is guaranteed to transform your thinking about faith. As you listen or watch, you will discover the difference between faith and hope. You will be presented with a definition of faith that will shed new light on both the Old and New Testaments. Andy Stanley explains what we can expect of God every time we come to him with a request. In addition, he exposes the flaws in what some have labeled The Faith Movement.

With both a DVD and separate participant's guide, *Faith, Hope, and Luck* is not just another group study. This content is foundational for everyone who desires to be an informed, active follower of Christ.

Five sessions include:

1. Better Odds
2. Betting on Hope
3. Beating the Odds
4. No Dice
5. All In

Available in stores and online!

ZONDERVAN®
.com

Five Things God Uses to Grow Your Faith

Andy Stanley

Imagine how different your outlook on life would be if you had absolute confidence that God was with you. Imagine how differently you would respond to difficulties, temptations, and even good things if you knew with certainty that God was in all of it and was planning to leverage it for good. In other words, imagine what it would be like to have PERFECT faith. In this DVD study, Andy Stanley builds a biblical case for five things God uses to grow BIG faith.

In six video sessions, Andy covers the following topics:
- Big Faith
- Practical Teaching
- Providential Relationships
- Private Disciplines
- Personal Ministry
- Pivotal Circumstances

Along with the separate participant's guide, this resource will equip groups to become more mature followers of Jesus Christ.

Available in stores and online!

Twisting the Truth

Learning to Discern in a Culture of Deception

Andy Stanley

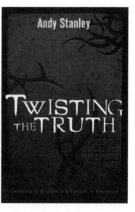

In six insight-packed sessions, Andy Stanley exposes four destructive and all-too-prevalent lies about authority, pain, sex, and sin. They're deceptions powerful enough to ruin our relationships, our lives, even our eternities—but only if we let them. Including both a small group DVD and participant's guide that work together, *Twisting the Truth* untwists the lies that can drag us down. With his gift for straight, to-the-heart communication, Andy Stanley helps us exchange falsehoods for truths that can turn our lives completely around.

Available in stores and online!

Share Your Thoughts

With the Author: Your comments will be forwarded to the author when you send them to *zauthor@zondervan.com*.

With Zondervan: Submit your review of this book by writing to *zreview@zondervan.com*.

Free Online Resources at

www.zondervan.com

Zondervan AuthorTracker: Be notified whenever your favorite authors publish new books, go on tour, or post an update about what's happening in their lives at www.zondervan.com/authortracker.

Daily Bible Verses and Devotions: Enrich your life with daily Bible verses or devotions that help you start every morning focused on God. Visit www.zondervan.com/newsletters.

Free Email Publications: Sign up for newsletters on Christian living, academic resources, church ministry, fiction, children's resources, and more. Visit www.zondervan.com/newsletters.

Zondervan Bible Search: Find and compare Bible passages in a variety of translations at www.zondervanbiblesearch.com.

Other Benefits: Register yourself to receive online benefits like coupons and special offers, or to participate in research.

ZONDERVAN®

ZONDERVAN.com/
AUTHORTRACKER
follow your favorite authors